BEST DAMN MARKETING TOOL EVER

Writing a Nonfiction Book to Grow Your Business

By
Donna Amos

Copyright © 2018 Donna Amos

All rights reserved. No part of this book may be used or reproduced by any means, graphic, electronic, or mechanical, including photocopying, recording, taping or by any information storage retrieval system without the written permission of the publisher except in the case of brief quotations.

Although every precaution has been taken to verify the accuracy of the information contained herein, the author and publisher assume no responsibility for errors or omissions. No liability is assumed for damages that may result from the use of information contained within.

Inspired Press Publisher
1333 Chelsea Court
Morrow, OH 45152
www.inspiredpresspublisher.com
513-256-1792

ISBN-13: 978-0-578-42289-3

Library of Congress Control Number: 2018965146

DEDICATION

This book is dedicated to my husband Mike.
Thank you for your support and encouragement.

TABLE OF CONTENTS

Introduction	vii
Why write a book for your business?	1
Understanding your why	13
Who are you writing for?	21
How to choose your topic	27
Reverse outline	37
Self-Sabotage	43
Establishing a writing habit	49
Beyond the first draft	59
Pre-publication	69
Getting noticed in a noisy world	75
Tools every writer can use	83
References	89

INTRODUCTION

Writing a book is a tremendous experience. It pays off intellectually. It clarifies your thinking. It builds credibility. It is a living engine of marketing and idea spreading, working every day to deliver your message with authority. You should write one.

Seth Godin

So, you have a goal to become a published author. That's awesome! How long have you had this goal? If you are like me, it's been years. Years spent imagining a goal, but with no system to achieve it, is really just wishing. After loads of research, reading, stopping and restarting, I found a system that worked for me. And I bet it'll work for you too.

Let's get started. You can start and finish your book in no time.

Access the resources at:
INSPIREDPRESSPUBLISHER.COM/RESOURCES

And use the code: Prosper

Chapter One

WHY WRITE A BOOK FOR YOUR BUSINESS?

You've probably noticed that a lot of business leaders and solopreneurs have started writing their own books. Some of those books even land on the *New York Times*' Bestseller's List. Writing a book and publishing it isn't easy, but you can make yourself stand out from competitors if you become a published author. Moreover, being a published author causes others to subconsciously view you as more knowledgeable, professional, and authoritative.

One of the biggest obstacles to writing your own book is overcoming the mental barrier that spouts writing a book is something you can't do or would do poorly. Such a damning, yet imaginary voice has stopped the fresh flow of ideas from many creative pens. Or keyboards. Solopreneurs, especially, struggle with this mental block. But it's really not as impossible as you might think. Some published authors will tell you that writing the book is the easy part; promoting it is the difficult task.

Consider this…

On a beautiful summer afternoon, five years ago, two men each launched new online businesses. They were very much alike. Both graduated from college, both had 10 years of business experience behind them, both were personable, and both were ambitious and held ambitious dreams for the future.

Recently, these men returned to their college for their 15th reunion. The similarities continued. Both were happily married, both had two children, and both were still in business.

But there was a difference. One of the men was extremely successful in his online business, more than doubling revenues every year. The other was still working hard month to month to generate the revenues he needed to support his family.

What Made The Difference?

Have you ever wondered, as I have, what makes this kind of difference in people's lives? It isn't always a native intelligence or talent or dedication. It isn't that one person wants success and the other doesn't. The difference lies in what each person knows and how he or she makes use of that knowledge.

Every business owner is an expert in their industry and should share that expertise with others. One of the ways to do so is by putting that knowledge into a book. A book expands your reach, builds an audience, and is a calling card for your business. You will instantly be seen as an expert who has answers to the questions your customers ask.

This book will provide the step-by-step instructions on how to determine your book topic, how to develop your chapters, and how to write consistently to complete your manuscript within six months.

About those two men I mentioned at the beginning of this chapter? They were college graduates, had business experience and launched their businesses at the same time.

So what made their business lives different?

Knowledge. Useful knowledge and its application. The most successful man put that knowledge in the form of a book. That book opened doors that helped attract new clients and build his business fast. The other man had often thought about writing a book but never followed through.

I can't promise you that success will be instantly yours if you start writing your book; after all, only 3 percent of the people that begin a book ever finish it. But I can promise that if you absorb the advice in this book and follow through, you will have the tools to make a difference in your business' success.

Don't let the difficult aspects of writing a book deter you. Instead, focus on the ways it will support and grow your business. That will help keep you excited when the going gets tough. Also remember you're not in it alone. You likely have an editor and publisher guiding you along the way. You could even find a mentor to guide you if you're still concerned about doing a good job.

5 Ways Writing Your Own Book Can Support Your Business

Here are five ways that writing your own book can support your business:

1. Earn New Customers and Loyal Fans

You will attract new customers and loyal fans when you publish a book. It can take someone longer to become a fan of your business when they just read your blog posts. Because published books are viewed as a much higher authority than blog posts, a person can more quickly become a fan of you or your business. If your book sparked their interest in your business, then they will look it up and buy one of your products or sign up for your e-course. They will want to gain the benefits of using your products, and they will also want to learn as much as possible from you. Through that process, they could become a fan of your brand.

What exactly does it mean to be a fan or brand advocate of your business? As defined by marketer Ross Beard on the Client Heartbeat blog, "Brand advocates are highly satisfied customers who go out of their way to actively promote the products they love and care about." The author of Brand Advocates, Rob Ruggetta, discovered through his research that a brand advocate is 50 percent more beneficial than the average customer. Here are some of the benefits you receive from brand advocates:

- Word-of-mouth marketing. Fans of your brand talk positively about your business to other people.
- An increase in positive online reviews of your business. Most customers don't take the time to write a review unless they were extremely satisfied or unhappy. Loyal fans of your business often leave a positive review to help you out and share their own excitement over the product.
- Customers that stay through the bad times. If they've become a fan, they'll stick through the good and bad times.
- Increased brand awareness.

2. Learn More about Yourself and Your Business

Another benefit of becoming a published author is you learn more about yourself and your business through the process. Book writing requires a lot of research, planning, and organization. You get to tap into your creativity as well find unique, engaging ways to present all the valuable information you have to share. Throughout all of these phases, you will learn more about yourself and your business. You will discover which topics excite you the most and which areas you're not that interested in mastering. It will help you fine-tune the services you offer as well as become clearer on what services you don't offer.

Remember that part of writing a business plan involves specifying who you won't serve and what services you won't offer. Knowing what you don't do is as important as knowing what you do. Who your target audience is becomes clearer. According to Tanya Hall, CEO of

Greanleaf Book Group, many people who approach her for help with book writing worry that they don't have enough material to write a book. After a few days of consultation, they realize they have the opposite problem: they have so much to write that they have to narrow it down for the book. They gain a greater understanding of their businesses and the processes they use in business that make them successful as a result of planning the book.

Personal organizer and author of "From Frazzled to Freedom" Julie Starr Hook admitted, "Writing my book forced me to look at my strengths and weaknesses." She discovered that she is naturally good at organizing bathrooms, kitchens, and offices, but she struggles with digital organization. "I recognized while writing this book that I don't have to specialize in every area," she shared.

Increase Your Credibility

When you write a book, your credibility increases. You can use this to your advantage by adding "author" to your social media bios and introducing yourself as an author. Erika Andersen shared in an article she wrote on Forbes that people perceived her as smarter and more expert after she became a published author People who wouldn't have listened to her before suddenly had an interest in what she had to say. Your business is viewed as more legitimate when you're a published author, too. Customers will buy from you with greater ease and trust.

New Opportunities Materialize

Many entrepreneurs who have written books said that an abundance of new opportunities came their way afterward. David Niu, author of Careercation and founder of TINYpulse, said that he received more speaking engagements after he added "author" to his bio. The increase in credibility directed more opportunities his way, and those opportunities helped promote and grow his business. Lori Matzke, owner of Center Stage Home and author of "Home Staging: Creating Buyer-Friendly Rooms to Sell Your House" has made several TV appearances since publishing her book. People also now consider her an expert in home staging.

Encourages Networking and Making More Connections

Another primary way that publishing a book helps your business is it pushes you to network and make more connections. It is likely that you'll end up interviewing or talking to at least one expert during the course of writing your book in order to provide facts and credibility. How many business books lack quotes or research from experts? Not many!

It's important to back up claims for readers to believe what you're saying and trust the information. Readers want to know when something is fact, theory, or opinion. Connecting with people at networking events is easier, too, when you can include being an author in your introduction. It gives you more credibility, allowing you to connect more easily with other experts in the industry. If you want to grow your business and receive new opportunities, writing a book is one of the best things you could do. You will learn more about yourself, your business, and your niche during the process. Once the book is published, you'll generate new leads for your business, earn new customers, and maybe even receive a few new fans. Solopreneurs who write their own books can reach a higher level in business that they wouldn't have otherwise reached.

Now if you are convinced that you should take the leap and get started writing, let's jump in.

10 Steps to Be Seen as an Expert

Do you think becoming an expert in your business niche requires countless thousands of hours of labor and experience? There was a time when this was the case in industry; and it may still ring true in certain pursuits. But in today's fast-paced digital world, deliberately focusing on some basic steps can gain you the expertise you need to become recognized as an expert in your chosen field in as little as 12 months. Does this seem too good to be true? Examine the steps below and follow them to increase your knowledge regarding your chosen topic.

Read Up On Your Topic

Internet shopping, purchase reviews, and digital books make searching for the top writers in any field a simple exercise. Choose the top works from recognized industry experts and read up on your topic. You can also ask for suggested works to read in industry forums and from other individuals in your circle of influence who are engaged in a similar business. Try to read at least 10 books on your chosen niche over the next 12 months.

Listen to Relevant Podcasts

Podcasts are an excellent way to leverage free time to learn more about a topic. Driving, exercising, or just relaxing over a cup of coffee can be prime times for listening and digesting information. Search for podcasts in your target business niche and follow the most highly rated podcasters. Listen to archived sessions as well as new content. The conversational approach podcasting takes to discussing issues and topics is a prime way to get relevant information in context and easily understood.

Follow the News of Your Business Niche

Subscribing to a few business news outlets is a key to staying current on all the relevant news in your chosen business niche. Scan articles daily and highlight any you wish to review when time permits. Add these articles to your reading time or scan them over lunch. News provides differing perspectives on trends, current events, surprise happenings, and industry leaders. Keeping current on the news in your business niche is a great way to bone up on knowledge of your chosen topic.

Follow Industry Experts

Every business and industry has experts who share their knowledge and observations. This can be through social media, blogs, magazine articles, company websites, and more. Discover the names that are repeated most often in your business niche and follow their blogs, writings, and social media accounts. They will likely have a great deal of free available information concerning your topic. Scan article topics and titles and bookmark relevant pieces for later reading.

Build Your Own Network with Others

Connect with industry leaders through the internet on sites like LinkedIn and reach out to them. Respect their time as busy professionals and begin small. Ask for a bit of their time and send a list of questions. If they respond favorably with answers, explore the possibility of a video call or face-to-face meeting to get to know them and their business story. As you get to know them, they will get to know you as well, and these connections can pay rich dividends in the future.

Join a Networking Association in Your Niche

Associations provide opportunities to network with industry professionals, participate in educational seminars, and gain relevant content on topics of interest to those in your business niche. You can meet with local experts and create connections for future learning and business opportunities. A surprising number of advances and profitable moves are made due to connections within networking communities.

Enroll in an Industry Course

Investing in educational seminars or courses offered by industry leaders is a prime way to immerse yourself in a topic. Some local community colleges may offer relevant courses for affordable prices. Another prime option is utilizing online sites that offer quick topic courses. Searching the internet for these may reveal many affordable options from which you may benefit greatly.

Attend Conferences and Trade Shows

Industry-sponsored conferences and trade shows are excellent opportunities to hear from and connect with top thinkers and leaders in seminars and training sessions. A plethora of learning and networking opportunities will be located in a single location and they are well worth your time to attend. In just a few days, you can learn from and connect with a host of leaders face to face instead of spending months pursuing these same individuals through more impersonal means.

Participate in Industry Advisory Groups

Most industry associations have advisory groups that offer numerous opportunities to impact and inform industry direction and regulation. Join one of these working groups and get to know other motivated members and their business agendas. You will gain valuable insight into the inner workings of your chosen business as well as receive first-hand knowledge of important trends and their effect on the industry at large as well as your own business.

Offer Your Business Knowledge to a Nonprofit Organization

Many nonprofit groups need access to industry experts but cannot afford to pay a fee for their expertise. As your knowledge grows, offer your services to these groups for free. You will gain an awareness of how these groups impact your industry as a whole as well as increase your knowledge of how nonprofits and your industry rely on one another. Your position as a business representative to the nonprofit can also open up important connections in your community and business niche, which can further establish you as an expert in your field.

Becoming an expert in your field cannot happen without effort. The steps above provide a framework for systematically increasing your knowledge and making important personal connections within your business niche. Following these steps can establish you as an expert in your field in as little as 12 months, but the process doesn't end after a single year. The business landscape is constantly changing, so making the above steps regular habits will ensure you stay at the top of your field as trends come and go and your business niche undergoes significant change.

What steps have you taken to become more knowledgeable in your field? Would you be considered an expert in your business niche? How did you gain that status?

BEST DAMN MARKETING TOOL EVER

"THE VERY LEAST YOU CAN DO IN YOUR LIFE IS TO FIGURE OUT WHAT YOU HOPE FOR. AND THE MOST YOU CAN DO IS LIVE INSIDE THAT HOPE. NOT ADMIRE IT FROM A DISTANCE BUT LIVE RIGHT IN IT, UNDER ITS ROOF."
~ BARBARA KINGSOLVER

CHECK OUT THE LIST OF RESOURCES AT
INSPIREDPRESSPUBLISHER.COM/RESOURCES

Chapter Two

UNDERSTANDING YOUR WHY

The biggest challenge with taking on writing a book is staying motivated to keep writing.

If you don't have a really strong why, and you haven't documented that, getting through the whole process can be very difficult. So just as a reminder, "He who has a why can endure any how."

How are you going to go from start to finish and actually complete your book? "He who has a why can endure any how." What that means, is if you have a really strong why for writing the book, then the how becomes much less tedious. We're going to cover your reasons, the passions that you have around a book topic, and reconnecting to the why when needed.

The only way you'll be able to write and finish your book is if you are continually reminding yourself why you wanted to write the book in the first place. It can't just be, "I want to make money." That's not a good enough reason. It won't motivate you to continue, so you need to zero in on the irreplaceable, irrefutable, undeniable reason why this book, on the topic that you choose, matters to you right now. You need to write that reason down in one to three sentences. Then I want you to read it every time, every single time you sit down to write.

You need to read that why in advance because procrastination can slip in there really fast. You have to continuously be reminded. Tape it to your computer screen, your mirror, your coffeepot, your TV, wherever you can see it often to keep reminding you that your book is more important than checking your email or turning on the news. Because any given day, you can think of a thousand reasons why you don't have the time to write the book and why you're not ready to do so. Therefore, make your why as strong as possible so it helps pull you through those times when you want to procrastinate.

When you're first sitting down to write your 'why this book is important to you' sentences, pay attention to your own emotions. If it takes you a long time to come up with a good reason, or if you feel weighed down and trapped when you're posting your why above your work place, then there's a problem. Writing and posting your why should actually lift your spirits and inspire you. So if writing is draining the process, then it's easy to lose sight of why you should return to your screens day after day, typing words that no one is yet reading. Although we're going to try to help with that as well.

But, bottom line, you must write them down and then place them where you'll see them often and read them every time you sit down to write. You see a pattern here? I think I've told you three times now, write 'em down, post 'em where you can see them. This really is an important step.

Why Do You Need a Why?

Now 16 - 20 weeks is a long time, and not that you're going to be writing that entire time, and you can certainly finish sooner than that; but there are a lot of steps along the way, so you don't want to lose your passion before you get completed.

Reconnecting with your why is the only way you're going to convince yourself to open that document again and again and type some more words. If you try to write out your why and post it, but you feel a sense of dread or obligation or dryness, then stop and reevaluate. Maybe you don't want to write a book, or maybe you do want to write a book, but it's not this book. As we go through this process of topics, you might decide the topic makes logical sense, but your heart just isn't in it. So, we would need to find you a new topic so your heart is in it and that it will make a difference in your business.

Many times writing that book is about making a contribution. So Brian Tracy says, "True happiness and fulfillment come when you feel that you are making a valuable contribution to the world." That could be one of the why's for you writing your book, is making that contribution to something that's important to you so that you can be the change. So if you could write a book that would change the world, what would it be about?

The reason you're going to write your book, is we want to set you up as the expert, so you're seen by your audience, your target market as the expert in your area, which will give you instant credibility. It will bring you more clients because they see you as an expert. It'll open up opportunities for speaking engagements. There's just a lot of ways that you can use it. And there are three kinds of experts. Each has his or her own right way of doing things and there is no right or wrong method. It's totally up to the individual.

The first is the researcher. The researcher is a diligent student and a lifelong learner. You learn what the top influencers in your field are doing and you report on it. The researcher's skill is synthesizing the information and packaging it in a way that is easy to understand.

The second type of expert is the results maker. A results maker is just that he or she is able to take information in their area of expertise and create a desired income. This expert gets better at explaining these results to others and he or she becomes the expert in the area because they're so good at explaining it.

Then finally there's the role model. The role model is the expert who gets results and helps guide others to them as well. This person is typically the leader of the tribe with respects and identifies with their perspective tribe. So having a tribe, it's not a prerequisite for this level, but more of a side effect that comes as a result of being the role model.

You may already see yourself in one of these areas or you may find along the way which one you're going settle into and feel really comfortable delivering the content as a researcher, or results maker, or a role model.

As you're writing, you're going to start with the message, the idea or the story that you really want to share with other people and this really needs to be something that you're passionate about.

Something that you believe in. Like we said, if your heart's not in it, then it will not be easy for you to show up and continue to write. When you're thinking about finding your content and what you're going to write about, there are some things to think about. Do you want to change the way people think? Or do you want to show them how to do what it is you teach? Do you want to be the teacher along the way, or do you want to motivate them as humans to join you with your cause? You know, higher levels of being. What is it that you want to accomplish? What are you trying to give back to your audience? That's the most important thing - providing value and giving back. Your book needs to be a resource to your audience. Later, we'll talk about the outcomes, what do you want them to do, what's the next step after they read your book, what's next?

I'm going to tell you that part of the challenge with becoming a writer, an author, is that you really don't have the confidence to declare yourself as a writer; or you fear that if you take the first step and actually commit to writing, that's a challenge. But I'm going to encourage you to let go of the fear. Fear is just paralyzing, it'll put you into procrastination, and that procrastination will look like valid reasons why you can't write. There will be a thousand of them, valid reasons, why you can't move forward, but it really is just fear disguised as valid reasons.

But I want to tell you that you are an author. You just have to choose, make the decision to do that. The truth is that successful authors, they struggle with what words to use and how to describe a concept and know what to write about next, just as much as the rest of us.

We're going to walk through some processes that are going to help you break down everything into such tiny bites, that picking up your keyboard to start writing again will be easy along the way. You'll have really specific pieces to write about rather than ambiguous thoughts. The worst thing to do is to say I'm going to write a book and sit down to start writing, and about three pages in, you don't know where to go next. We don't want that to happen.

There is a myth that authors have this special God-given, divinely-inspired talent that enables them to put words and phrases together effortlessly. We kind of romanticize writers in that respect. But if you talk to any, whether they're writing novels or writing non-fiction, any author will tell you they struggle, that there are times when it just isn't working for them. The difference is that they continue to write even though they're not sure how to describe a concept or what they're going to write about next. They just continue to write. If they have to put dot, dot, dot and move on, they do, and then they come back to it at a later time to fill in the dot, dot, dot.

That's important to remember: those writers aren't perfect. The only reason they may be better at it then we are, is that they do it more often. So, it's practice, just like anything else. Whether you're an athlete or an author or a physician. Everything takes practice. You don't become a great heart surgeon by doing it once.

Your Journal

Here's what you're going to do. Get a journal. I know you're going to do most everything on your computer, but I want you to get a journal so you can put every thought and action and any little quote you might find, into that journal. Keep it with you at all times. You will find there are times that something you think is genius will come to you, and if you don't write it down, you're not going to remember it. Your journal is the vessel you'll use to draw or jot something down or map out an idea. It's just easier to have that journal handy. Don't mix it up with the other things you have to do. Don't include your normal to-do list, because it'll get lost and it won't have the same meaning.

Now you're not going to write everything in this journal, but I do want you to put something in it. And I would like for you to put on the label, the spine, the title, because then it feels kind of official. It's your working title, it's not what you're going to decide in the end, but your title there, or put your why there and make sure that you have it with you, because you're going to need it along the way.

Your Outcome

Let's talk about the desired outcome for your book. You're writing this book to help grow your business, so what's the highest and the greatest outcome? I want you to dream really big here and make it scary, because big, bodacious goals help pull us forward. But, understand that those really big dreams are fulfilled by taking small steps. Visualize this: a reader has your book and they have finished it. What is it that you want them to do next? You'll include a call to action in the front and back of your book to tell them what you want them to do next. And you only include one call to action, so readers don't become confused.

Some authors include instructions on how to get a workbook that goes with their book. That could be a good way to build an email list for later campaigns. You can then invite them to attend workshops or other things. Or do you want them to spread the word about your book or cause? If yours is a cause that you want and need people to become passionate about, then you might want them to buy another copy and give it to a friend. That might be the best outcome that you can have, to get it in front of more people. Do you want them to spend thousands of dollars to work with you? That certainly is an option as well, and for some consultants that work with big companies, that can absolutely be the result of them seeing you as the expert in your industry. As long as we get the marketing right along the way, so that your message is consistent.

Part of your assignment this week is to think about what you want readers to do after reading your book. What is the next step for them to take? Most of the time, it will be a small step. So, think about that. What is the desired outcome of someone reading your book.

Summary

Here is what you're going to do for this chapter. Document your why. Buy that journal. Identify the outcome that you want for your book.

BEST DAMN MARKETING TOOL EVER

"IF YOUR DREAM IS A BIG DREAM, AND IF YOU WANT YOUR LIFE TO WORK ON THE HIGH LEVEL THAT YOU SAY YOU DO, THERE'S NO WAY AROUND DOING THE WORK IT TAKES TO GET YOU THERE."
--JOYCE CHAPMAN

CHECK OUT THE LIST OF RESOURCES AT
INSPIREDPRESSPUBLISHER.COM/RESOURCES

Chapter Three

WHO ARE YOU WRITING FOR?

Let's start with your target market. This is the key to success. You really do have to keep them top of mind when you're writing your book. As you're determining your chapters and your topic initially, and then the chapters within that topic, you always have to keep in mind who are you writing for? What is it that you want to share with them, and is it something they have an interest in?

It would not be fun if we were writing something about which we think our target market would have an interest, but they actually do not. So, some of the things that we're going to talk about can help determine that.

It could be really helpful to identify a profile for your target market. What are their hopes, their fears, their dreams? What's motivating them? What's their interests or their concerns? What are the problems of your reader that your book will solve? If you can focus on that, you'll have a winner.

Identifying Your Target Market

Focus on one person to which you are writing. Determine everything there is to know about that person, and keep them in mind as you are writing. Once you know who you're writing for, and the problem that you're solving, that helps with your book's topic.

Research your target market's demographics. The following is important information:

- Age
- Gender
- Income level
- Career
- Education
- Life stage
- Family status
- Location

All of those things are important in identifying their interests, their challenges, and how you can help support them in identifying the problem they have so you can provide a solution.

Next, examine their psychographics. What are their favorite books? Who are their favorite authors? What genres do they read most often? Are they loyal to that genre? How many books do they read per month? Do they read mainly for work or for pleasure? What kind of movies or television programs do they watch regularly? How do they spend their free time? What are their hobbies? What kind of vacations do they like the best? Do they prefer to stay at home? What are their buying habits? Do they make impulse purchases or do they hunt for great deals? Do they rely on recommendations from friends?

Study their online behavior to discover what blogs they enjoy reading. What are the social media sites where they spend the most time? Are they Candy Crush kind of people on Facebook, or do they spend their time on Pinterest pinning and saving? Where do they shop the most? Are they online shoppers or do they prefer to go into the store?

Do they visit forums? How about Google groups or Facebook groups? Or maybe Reddit? Identifying the forums and the groups where they hang out will help you to know where to go to ask the questions you need to ask. It's good to go out to your audience and ask them questions. Make certain you are providing a solution to a real problem they face.

Google and Google AdWords are great places to look for insights and trends. Enter keywords and see how that keyword is trending on Google. Work with Google AdWords keyword planner and search for those keywords that you believe are appropriate to your book and the questions for which your audience is searching. Then take those keywords and go to trends and see how they perform there.

Visit a website called Answer the Public. It can show you lists of questions searchers are using on Google for different keywords. That can really help you, if you see that there's a handful of questions that are being asked, then you might want to look at the chapters you have chosen for your book and make certain that you answer those questions within your chapters. If not, make some changes to your chapters to make certain that you can answer those questions.

Facebook insights on your page and inside business manager are very helpful, as is Twitter analytics. Each of these will give you additional information about your followers, and that can help you make some good decisions about your book.

Cultivating an Audience

This is also a great way to identify blog topics that you can start writing about while you're writing your book. You can begin educating your audience along the way, showing them some of your expertise. Make them want to know more. Consider even sharing the first chapter of your book as a teaser for future sales. Ask readers to sign up for a waiting list for the entire book. Start building your mailing list now, if you don't already have one. It will be a vital tool later in marketing.

Summary

For this chapter, do a dig deep into your target market in order to identify their most pressing problems. Get their feedback; tell them why you're asking. People love to be part of something.

Next, we will really get focused on the topic. How do you choose? We'll talk through four different ways that you can determine your topic. One of the four ways will work for you. I promise.

BEST DAMN MARKETING TOOL EVER

"THERE IS ONLY ONE WINNING STRATEGY. IT IS TO CAREFULLY DEFINE THE TARGET MARKET AND DIRECT A SUPERIOR OFFERING TO THAT TARGET MARKET."
~PHILIP KOTLER

CHECK OUT THE LIST OF RESOURCES AT
INSPIREDPRESSPUBLISHER.COM/RESOURCES

Chapter Four

HOW TO CHOOSE YOUR TOPIC

If writing a book for your business as a solopreneur, you will want to choose a topic that resonates with you as well as with your target audience. A book that scratches where others have an itch will catch on and be imminently useful to a wide audience. Such a work will establish you as an authority on your chosen topic and drive consumers to your business.

Great writing is always about something. Likely, you already have a topic in mind or you wouldn't be considering a book. Why did you choose this topic? Why and how will it grab readers' attention? Write the basic premise of your book in one sentence. Then, explain it in a paragraph. Very likely, you will discern some natural steps or divisions in your explanation. This will be the beginning of your working outline.

Construct a Basic Outline

From the explanatory paragraph you wrote above, establish a basic one-page outline. Every story must go somewhere. If you aim at nothing you are guaranteed to hit it every time. If your topic is related to business, most likely it will require a systematic explanation that is easy for readers to follow. This is where an outline is crucial.

After writing out a working outline, construct a table of contents. Each section could be a chapter, or a division with several chapters in each. This is labeled a working outline because, just like your writing, it is a work in progress. As you begin writing you may discover that some sections demand more detail or explanation and will require more space. Change your outline and table of contents to reflect any revisions in the book's framework.

You might want to remember that journal that we talked about purchasing, because it can be a great place to do the brainstorming that we're going to talk about. You don't have to put pen to paper, though. If you're more comfortable with the keyboard, then absolutely open up a Word document and type away, because there's no right or wrong way.

There is a software product called Scrivener, it started for fiction, but it's really helpful for non-fiction as well. It helps you organize your chapters, put in notes and research all in one place. It could be helpful in the process, but a lot of people use a Word document, and maybe Dropbox or Evernote, so they can clip things when they're doing research. Whatever works for you is fine.

4 Ways to Determine Your Topic

Let's start with the four ways that you can determine the best topic for your book. At least one of these methods will work best for you. I challenge you to try them all, then see which way seems the most profitable for you.

Free Writing

Free writing is getting that pen and paper, or your keyboard, setting a timer for 10 minutes, and asking yourself the question, "What will my book be about?" Simply ask the question, and then write down literally everything that comes to mind. No editing. Something may come to mind that you think is totally ridiculous. It doesn't matter. Write everything down and don't do any kind of editing, just write as many items as fast as you can.

Remember that if you've been thinking about writing this book for a while, your mind has actually been working as you attempt to go to sleep at night, or take a shower, or waiting in the supermarket. There are ideas that are just waiting to find their way out and onto paper, and this is their chance to do that. Your only job is to write fast enough during the 10 minutes to make sure you get all the ideas down on paper.

So, brainstorming can be really, really effective, but you do have to set a timer. If 10 minutes is not enough for you, then set it for 30 minutes, but the point is not to just sit there and think about things; you have to write. Anything that comes to mind in the beginning.

You might ask yourself if you didn't get the answer with that question, "What should my book be about?" then you might say, "What sparks my interest?" Or, "What gets me really excited?" If you have something that you really feel passionate about, you'll think about that topic, and you'll enjoy writing about it.

If you have to dive in and do more research, you'll enjoy doing the research. It will not feel forced, because you're passionate about the topic itself. That can be the other questions that you ask yourself, and then again, the brainstorming, just letting it all come out, and writing as fast as you can.

If neither of those work, then here's another way that you can use the brainstorming, and that is to think about your interests, your experiences, and any job-related knowledge that you have. By that means you ask yourself, "What am I interested in? What are my hobbies? I've always wanted to write about ... The reason I want to write this book is ... My favorite topic is ... I know a lot about ..."

Those are kind of interest questions. Find the things that you're interested in, or you can focus on your experience. You don't have to be an expert in that topic yet, because you can do the research that will help to bring you along; you just have to have some experience in it.

If you finish the sentences, "I have experience in ... I can definitely teach people about ... My experience allowed me to learn ..." Or, "My unique personal experience was ..." Those are the kind of questions that will help you to determine what kind of topics you could write about as it relates to your experience.

Then finally, job related. If you have past experience in your work life, whether it was working for yourself or for someone else, those lessons learned can be a great topic for your book.

You might start by saying, "When I worked at ... I learned about ..." Or, "In my profession, I know a lot about ... I want to be known as a leading expert in ... One area of my business people need to know about is ... I could write a book related to the topic of my business because if I wrote a book on it, I could impact more lives. My experience working in ..." So insert your profession there.

"My experience working in accounting could teach people more precisely about managing their money." Or, "Since I work in blank, people would benefit from my knowledge of blank." So think about those things. What have you done in your work life that you can share, that you have knowledge of, that you may choose to do research to become even more attached or aware of it, but ...

That's just option one, free writing. That can help you to just get things out of your brain and on paper so you can then start to narrow it down.

Choose An Area of Expertise

You can also choose to write something that's aligned with your business. If you possess some expertise in an area, by virtue of your experience in the industry, then that could be a natural choice for a topic. As an expert, you write a book. The book, in turn, gives you even more credibility as an expert. Books open doors. That's why I call it the best damn marketing tool ever.

Let's say you're a physician. You could write a book about patient stories over the last however many years you've been a physician, or you could write a story about heart surgery, and how to prevent a heart attack. If you looked in your general area, you'd probably find that of all the doctors within a 50 mile radius, none of them have written a book. If you want to stand out, then the best option for you would be to write that book about how to prevent a heart attack, because that sets you up as an expert with your patients, and will help you stand out among the other doctors in your area.

Once you've determined the subject matter, then go to Amazon and do a search to determine if there's actually a need for the topic. If there are some works, but the market doesn't seem saturated, then you have likely determined a good niche within your industry to be writing about.

Search Amazon for What's Currently Popular

This is a simple way to locate trending topics. Search on Amazon for trending topics that may interest you. If a topic is trending and you can get in on it, then that can be very helpful to being recognized.

If you think about health and fitness, relationships, time management, stress management, and money making strategies, those are the most searched for self-help categories in Amazon. Now, maybe you won't fit in there, but there may be another topic close to your business interests. Search in Amazon and see what comes up as the best sellers in the topic that you have an interest in, and see if it makes sense for you to write that book.

Then take note of the themes that are common among those best sellers. That could be a good place to get started. For example, in the health and fitness genre, you may find that juicing is a popular aspect of healthy dieting. If it is a common theme for writers, that means it's probably trending. Think about how you could write on that topic from a different perspective, one that may not be addressed in the current top sellers.

Remember, even though it's trending and there could be a lot of books written about it, competition is a good thing, because it shows you people are interested in that subject. It's okay. If you did a search for, "How many people write on sales," it's incredibly broad and crowded, very crowded, but everybody has a place, so it's okay.

Use Amazon to Locate Missed Topics

Here's another way to use Amazon to come up with the ideas for your book. Go to the category in which you have an interest. For example, let's use sales. Look at the books that have two- and three-star ratings. Read what is said in those ratings. Look for comments that ask further questions or identify something the reader wished the book had covered.

That reveals a gap in what the popular books cover. If you can locate those gaps, and address them in your book, those are great topics that will find traction with a wide audience. You can also check the table of contents for books already in that category to see what has been dealt with extensively and what has not.

Now determine what your topic is, and then look at that topic and come up with 10 to 15 independent topics that should go underneath it as sub-topics. You want to make certain that you're filling a gap that's been left by other authors. Once you have those independent topics, its time for another brainstorming session. This can actually become the basic outline for your book, arranged in a logical order.

Then you're going to repeat this. Divide up the 10 to 15 sub-topics, now go back, do another brainstorming session, and take the first independent topic and do the same thing. If you go down at least four levels under each sub-heading, you have a great basic outline for the entire book.

This can take you several days to actually get through, so it's not a fast process, but it will be extremely helpful when you start writing. Know that it's not written in stone; you're going to change it up. You're also going to find that you may need to do some research as you develop that outline, and that's okay, you don't have to do the research immediately.

You can start writing, and then when you need that research, then you can go and do it at that time. If you're not thrilled about actually writing or doing the research immediately, but you are excited about getting started on your writing, then do that, because that'll keep you excited and engaged in the process. Wait on the research until it's convenient.

Generate a Great Title

You need a great title in order for your book to be marketable. It's the phrase that people are going to say, over and over, when recommending your book to friends or talking about it on blogs. When you define a great title that is easy to remember, then you have tackled half of the marketing battle.

The goal of the title is to reveal your book's main concept. For a non-fiction book title, writing a good title means crafting a concrete promise, a clear benefit statement as to what the reader can expect to learn. Remember that you want your keyword in the title as well; it is your sales message.

These are the kind of titles that make a promise:

- *The 4-Hour Workweek*
- *How to Cook Everything*
- *What to Expect When You're Expecting*
- *20 Years Younger*
- *9 Steps to Financial Freedom*

You also get a sub-title for non-fiction books.

Come up with 10-20 potential titles. Pick your three favorites. Now go down this list and ask the following questions to see if it's marketable:

- Is this title easy to remember?
- Does it reveal the main concept or type of experience my book has to offer?
- Does the title express what type of reader will benefit from reading the book?
- Does the title provoke an impulse purchase?
- Would readers enjoy recommending this title to friends because it's fun, cool, or sexy? (word-of-mouth friendly)
- Does the title start a conversation when people hear it for the first time?
- Would it be easy to turn this title into a franchise? (Harry Potter and the..., The 4-Hour...)
- Is the domain available? (convenient, but not required)
- Are there any other books or copyrighted material with this same title?

If you answered "No" to some of those questions, keep brainstorming. Eventually, you'll hit upon a winning title.

BEST DAMN MARKETING TOOL EVER

"I DO BELIEVE SOMETHING VERY MAGICAL CAN HAPPEN WHEN YOU READ A BOOK."
~J.K. ROWLING

CHECK OUT THE LIST OF RESOURCES AT
INSPIREDPRESSPUBLISHER.COM/RESOURCES

Chapter Five

REVERSE OUTLINE

How can creating a reverse outline help and how do you create it? You're not going to need this until you finish that first draft, but it's good to understand how this will help you, because it might actually give you some peace of mind knowing there's a process for improving your draft, your manuscript, once you've got that first draft done. So, it really can help you to make a stronger structural manuscript using a reverse outline.

Here's kind of what the timing does. If you stay consistent, you can finish writing your manuscript in about 16 weeks. At the end of that 16 weeks, set it aside for a week. Next, do an initial read through, and during that read through, you're going to develop your reverse outline. That'll take you two to four days to complete. Once you've done that, then you'll go back and you'll do your first revision based on what you discovered doing the reverse outline. So that first revision will take approximately one week, ten days at the longest.

Four Methods of Creating a Reverse Outline

There are four ways to create your reverse outline, and none of them are right or wrong, it's just preference. It's what you prefer to do.

- Topic sentence
- One-sentence summary

- Two-sentence subject and function
- Idea by idea

Let's look at each one of these individually.

Topic Sentence

If every paragraph's first sentence, or topic sentence, provides a really succinct version of the paragraph's argument, then you're likely working with effective topic sentences in your book, and it'll be easy for you to do. So, on a computer, you'll just copy and paste the first sentence of each paragraph onto a separate document, or you'll hand-write it if you're doing longhand. So, the first sentence of each paragraph is put into a separate document. That's the topic sentence method.

One-Sentence Summary

If the first sentence in each paragraph isn't really an overview of the main point of the paragraph, or if it's a transition sentence, then for each paragraph, produce a one-sentence summary. Read the paragraph and write one sentence that summarizes what that paragraph is about. The sentence should express the main point of that paragraph. Again, put it in a separate document, following the order of the paragraphs in your book. That's the one-sentence summary.

Two-Sentence Summary and Function

Next there's the two-sentence approach, and some writers prefer this because it's more detailed. The first sentence shows the paragraph's subject or its topic, and then the second sentence shows the paragraph's function. Is it to compare, to propose, to describe, to set up a cause? That's just to name a few things that the function could be. Then you also want to number and order them as they appear in the book, so that you can easily identify each paragraph based on your two sentences, your subject and your function.

Idea by Idea

Finally, there is the idea by idea method. Sometimes it's useful to work through, if it's a challenging draft, by parsing out the ideas in each paragraph. Often, this comes in handy when you've used previous content that you've written, and you've done a combination of pulling in other content you've written to supplement it. This idea by idea method can help make certain that your flow and structure are working well. So, it is helpful for challenging drafts. You might call these "units of thought," so in each paragraph, you want to identify what the main idea is in that paragraph, and you want to make certain that you aren't just listing words or partial thoughts; you have to express it as a complete sentence. So, what is the idea of that paragraph? And it's okay if there's more than one idea; write them both down. You need to know the idea in each paragraph.

Evaluation

Now that you've done the hard work, you've got it all written out, take those new documents that have all of those sentences, and you use it to really evaluate your manuscript. Count your paragraphs and consider the ratio of paragraphs to written pages. Consider how long sentences are; they should be anywhere from five words to 40 words, but they shouldn't all be 25 words. There should be a variety in length and composition. If you tend to write really long sentences, this will help you to identify those and make certain you break them into easier-to-read lengths.

By comparing the total paragraphs to the total pages, you can learn your average paragraph length, and you'll know right away whether your paragraphs are too long, too short, or just right. There should be a good mix, not all the same.

Now that you've identified what each paragraph is about, then you can begin evaluating the overall structure and argument. Knowing your focus and message, have you missed an argument? In the structure you're using, make certain that it shows the most effective approach to writing about your book's subject. You might have to switch things up, or it may turn out that it's perfect. It also will help you to review your book's organization and structure, and then you can make strategic choices about rearranging the book on a paragraph-by-paragraph basis, or for adding paragraphs, combining or removing paragraphs to help improve the organization of your book.

Remember, the only adjustment that you're going to do with this outline is the structure of your manuscript, which means you're staying at the paragraph level. You're not going to adjust individual sentences yet, you're not going to adjust the wording, or even the spelling. You've got to ignore all of that. If you get sucked into details, you won't be able to maintain a broad overview of the manuscript, and that needs to be the first thing that you do. Get that broad overview, make certain that everything is structurally sound, and then you can move on to the editing process.

Writing

At this point, you should have all of your chapters identified, and you should be writing. If you're not writing, then it's time to start. To make certain that it happens, get out your calendar and schedule the time you're going to write. Get a timer, set it each day and write the full time you have allotted. But you have to start writing now. Now, now, now's the time.

How many words a week do you need to write? The average nonfiction book is between 40,000 and 60,000 words, so if you're at that 40,000 words, you should be able to complete your book in 16 weeks. That means you'll write 2,500 words in a week, or 500 a day. If you're at that 60,000 words, then it may take you 18 weeks, or you'd stretch it to 20 weeks if you wanted to stay with that same 2,500 words a week. But in 18 weeks, you could write 3,750 words a week and be complete in that 18 weeks with your 60,000 words, or 750 words per day.

BEST DAMN MARKETING TOOL EVER

"PERMANENCE, PERSEVERANCE AND PERSISTENCE IN SPITE OF ALL OBSTACLES, DISCOURAGEMENTS, AND IMPOSSIBILITIES: IT IS THIS, THAT IN ALL THINGS DISTINGUISHES THE STRONG SOUL FROM THE WEAK."
~ THOMAS CARLYLE

CHECK OUT THE LIST OF RESOURCES AT
INSPIREDPRESSPUBLISHER.COM/RESOURCES

Chapter Six

SELF SABOTAGE

Don't forget: "He who has a why can endure any how."

This is about the time you will start self-sabotaging yourself. I'm going to encourage you not to give in. Let's talk about a few ways that you can get around it. Once you begin your project and you're excited, you'll get up early to write, you'll skip your lunch to write, and you'll stay up late to write. You're so excited you can't stop thinking about the book. It's an obsession, like when you're a teenage girl, and you're obsessed over a boy. The fact is that you just can't get the book off your mind, and that's great, that's exciting.

Then, the newness wears off. You start feeling trapped. You'll want to put off writing the book, but then you'll feel guilty because you're not writing. Then, all of a sudden, the book has a life all its own. Eventually, you'll actually start resenting the fact that you started the project in the first place. Because that resentment has kicked in, and it's following the guilt, you'll want to procrastinate even more. You need to be aware that this is probably going to happen, so you can work around it and continue to move forward with writing your book. This can happen anywhere from three days to three weeks into your process.

This is what happens: you start turning excuses into valid reasons to give yourself permission not to follow through. Your self-talk kicks in, telling yourself, "You just don't have the time," or, "You shouldn't be writing in the first place. Who are you to think that you should be writing a book?" All those things, all those excuses you justify, and turn them into valid reasons why you shouldn't continue.

The only way you will write and finish this book is if you stay connected to your why.

Why is this book important to you? In the beginning when we worked on your why, what emotions did that why bring up for you? Hopefully, they were all good, positive emotions because, if you continue to remind yourself about the why, those emotions will help to pull you forward. For myself, my why would be I'm writing this book to encourage and inspire small business owners to stop procrastinating and give them the tools they need to write their book.

Go back and evaluate your why. Make sure that it's strong enough to keep you motivated and inspired to move forward. Then make sure you're reviewing it every day. You really have to just stay focused on it because that's the only way you're going to pull through.

One of the things that'll start happening is you want to go hide in a corner and write. You don't want to share with anybody until your manuscript is just perfect, before it's in a place where you think you won't get judged. That's the bottom line. Well, you need some support along the way. You need at least one person who believes in you like you should believe in yourself, someone that'll give you words of hope, that'll read anything that you ask them to, and they'll provide encouragement.

Then, it's also important to have another support person who will read your drafts and give you thoughtful, constructive, and even specific negative feedback. They're not giving you negative feedback about you or about your writing style. They're giving you feedback about the content, so you can create a manuscript that is better than you ever dreamt it could be. Some people are lucky enough to have one person that can play both those roles, but not always. If you don't have those two people in your life, then hire a coach or an editor to help you as you're moving along. It can be extremely powerful, and having somebody to share with is really important.

Here's the next thing you need to do. You need to give yourself permission to be a writer. Allow yourself to be that writer. Let it become part of your identity. If you're a writer, then you'll commit to the actual writing itself. Give yourself the title and claim it. Do things like add it to your LinkedIn title. Put it out there. In your LinkedIn title it says writer or author. Put it out there so that you start taking ownership of that title and giving yourself permission to be a writer.

Here's what happens in between our two ears. You start asking yourself if you can really be an expert in the topic that you've chosen. The real question you should be asking yourself is, can you provide value to your readers? Who decides whether somebody is an expert or not? It's about giving the reader value so they thought it was a good investment and idea for them to spend time reading your book. Those questions we start asking ourselves are the key to self-sabotage. It's because the fears and thoughts we have around those subjects. If you're fearful that someone will challenge whether you're an expert in your topic, or that you'll get judged in any other way, you need to turn that around and really just focus on the fact that you're bringing value to the reader. You have information to share that will be of value to them, that will help them to take that next step in whatever it is that you're helping them with.

One of the most powerful ways to destroy self-limiting beliefs is through positive self-talk. Again, I know that sounds simple, but it really is. Instead of saying, "Why bother?" say, "I'm bothering because I'm going to bring value to my readers," or, "I am going to do something with my writing, and it's going to be impactful to those that read it." Rewrite all of those negative statements that are going on in your head, and change the way you speak to yourself.

This is important because the self-sabotage will prevent you from finishing your book. You should have your initial chapters identified.

You shouldn't be ready to start writing, you should be writing. You should be writing right now. Now you're looking at finishing that first draft in 8 to 12 weeks. Isn't that pretty exciting? If you wrote last week, and you start putting that 1000 words a day on paper this week, then, you're going to be so much further along.

BEST DAMN MARKETING TOOL EVER

"SELF-SABOTAGE IS WHEN WE SAY WE WANT SOMETHING AND THEN GO ABOUT MAKING SURE IT DOESN'T HAPPEN."
~ ALYCE CORNYN-SELBY

CHECK OUT THE LIST OF RESOURCES AT
INSPIREDPRESSPUBLISHER.COM/RESOURCES

Chapter Seven

ESTABLISHING A WRITING HABIT

An old Spanish proverb speaks powerfully to the habit of writing: **"Habits are first cobwebs, then cables."**

How often have you began to set a regular practice of writing only to brush through the cobwebs holding you and never go back to it? Many aspiring writers struggle with this; in fact, anyone trying to accomplish creative work struggles to form the regular habit that leads to success and even greatness. If the thin cobwebs holding you to your writing habit are to become strong cables, you must take steps to integrate your passion into the habit.

I know it is difficult. I know you are likely very busy. I know YOU know you *should* be writing on a regular schedule. We both know there are also many other things you *should* be doing:

- Drink more water
- Spend more time exercising
- Spend more time doing homework
- Enjoy more time with your family
- Floss and brush your teeth longer
- Learn another language
- Plant a tree
- Get that yearly physical
- Wash the dog

- Call your mother more often
- And you can add to the list…

How do you carve out room for your writing when all these other important things are clamoring for your attention?

Set a Written Commitment

Make a serious commitment and set it all down on paper. When and where, for how long, and everything else that pertains to your habit. Write it down. Make a personal contract with yourself and date it. Post it where it can give you daily motivation as you write. You are a writer; now adhere to your commitment and write. As you begin a new writing project, consider composing a new contract specific to the new work, with a beginning date and firm commitments until completion.

Write Every Day

Opinions abound concerning this, and debate will never cease. Don't waste time on the discussions pro and con – just set a time and place to write every day and write. Every. Day. Period. Be honest; we all find time to do the things we deem important to us. If writing is as important to you as you think, say, or claim, then carve out the time and do it. Every day. Eliminate other lesser pursuits, shove things that can wait aside, and write. How long isn't as important, at least in the beginning. Fifteen minutes every day is better than nothing.

Set a Trigger

A trigger is an event that sets off your habit. Many smokers indulge when they wake, when stressed, or when eating. Those actions or events are the trigger. To create a new habit, you need to associate your habit with a trigger. If you write in the morning, you may associate it with going to the bathroom or your morning cup of coffee. An evening writing habit might be associated with doing the dishes after the evening meal. Choose a trigger you know you will do every day as a routine, and connect your writing time to it.

Get Accountability Partners

Share your new writing habit with others and ask them to hold you accountable. Tell your family and friends, co-workers, other writer friends, post it on your blog. Commit publicly and explain what you will do, and further commit to report on a regular basis. Give a few trusted people permission to call or text at random times and check up on you, or provide some needing encouragement. Accountability is a vital step to forming any important practice, including your writing habit.

Commit to a 30-Day Focus

A vital aspect of forming any habit is focus. If you place your full, undivided focus on forming this habit, you will likely succeed. Set a 30 day period and focus relentlessly on your writing habit. Don't try anything else new during this period. Don't allow anything to diffuse your focus. If necessary, let other things go. After all, it's just 30 days; the laundry will still be there. Seriously, make your writing habit the absolute top priority for that month. The focus you learn will carry over into the next days and months.

Keep a Writing Log

Get a calendar or create a spreadsheet for the sole purpose of recording your writing. Record your time spent writing, and a short note about what was accomplished. Remember your accountability partners? Share your progress with them as well. Post a short entry on your blog or social media immediately after you perform the habit. The concrete record will motivate you to carry on, especially when others become accustomed to seeing your update. Write daily, log it, and share it.

Reward Yourself

Set some writing goals and celebrate when you reach them. It could be a week of writing every day or a certain word count reached. Create milestones and even brainstorm and designate how you will reward yourself when you reach each one. This is key motivation to keep going. A writer I know recently rewarded himself with a retreat to a beautiful coastal island for a week of relaxation and writing. Start small with a nice dinner out or a pair of new jeans. Make each goal tougher and each reward more fulfilling.

Constantly Look for Inspiration

The best motivation is inspiration. What inspires you to write? Perhaps reading about other successful writers and their habits. Some find certain types of music to provide inspiration or spark artistic expression. Find a topic you feel strongly about and let that emotion motivate you to write. Discover an important spiritual connection and express your joy and satisfaction through writing. Research a cause that is near and dear and write about it.

Have Fun

Discipline doesn't have to be drudgery. Without some fun, you will lose the motivation to continue your writing habit. Experiment with different types of music and see how it affects your creativity. Enjoy your favorite coffee or tea while you write. Wear your favorite writing jammies. Meet with some friends for a time of brainstorming and writing. Take your writing to new and different locations, coffee shops, restaurants, or outdoor spaces. Enjoy a new environment and write about it. A friend of mine recently spent time writing while sitting in the middle of a corn maze!

What happens if you screw up and miss a day? Well, it's not time for the ball and chain just yet. Think about what caused you to miss, and find a solution so it doesn't happen again. Report your failure to your accountability partners (yes, call it a failure; failure isn't final) and keep going. With persistence, even the snail reached Noah's Ark.

Great Writing Tools

We're going to talk about writing habits and some of the tools available to help you to go from beginning to end. Will you write on a laptop, on a tablet, on your desktop, at work if you have different locations? You need to think about this, because if you use too many devices, then it'll become very muddled. It'll create problems for you. I wouldn't use more than two. If you write on your laptop at home and you write on the desktop at work, you've got two devices that you're using. You'll need to use Google Docs, or Evernote, or something where you can share that content so you're not redoing work from one device to the other.

Then you have to decide, how are you going to write? This is not something you can spend hours or days thinking about. This is not something to get hung up on. Are you going to use Word? Are you going to use Scrivener? Are you going to use Google Docs? Maybe you liked putting pen to paper, so you're going to write your book longhand, or you're going to speak your book into a recording device. These last two, if that's how you're going to write, which is fine, just make certain you have somebody else that's going to transcribe, or type out your notes, your long hand. That's not your job. Your job is to keep writing.

Writing Plan B

Make sure you have a plan B. If you didn't write in the morning, you're going to write at your desk during lunch, another 30 minutes. But then that can be interrupted, too. A colleague can want you to go to lunch. You might have to step out into a meeting. So, that doesn't always work. So, what's your plan C? Plan C would be you're back at home, you're going to write on your laptop for 30 minutes before you go to bed in the evening.

If you decide you're going to write daily, then create plans like this. Determine your options. I'm either going to write in the morning, I'm going to write during lunch, or I'm going to write before I go to bed. That will help keep you on track. If you just allow yourself to go with, "Well, when I have time. When I get 30 minutes during my day, I'll write," it'll never happen. So think of your plan. Where, when, on what device are you going to do your writing, so that you can take your book to the finish line.

Free Writing Exercise

You have in your head all the information you need to write your book. You've been immersed in your topic for a long time. That information is there. Now, you might need to do some research, but your brain contains more thoughts and information, associations and ideas than you could ever sort through by making a concerted effort.

But, using free writing you can get a lot closer. The free writing allows you to just write, with no expectations that you'll ever produce anything that is really useful. It doesn't have to be. Because the point of free writing is that it will open up what you need to do. What's going through your head? It'll open that up, so that you can get it out onto paper. It'll make your actual writing easier to do, because you freed your brain. You've told it, I'm only going to do this for a short time, and then we're going to go back to the normal way that we write.

Free writing is a great tool to help your mind access the information you already possess. Here's the basic steps to doing free writing. If you're writing session is 30 minutes in the morning, then 5, 10, 20 minutes prior to that session, do some free writing. You do that by setting a timer. That's very critical, setting the timer. Then you put pen to paper, or you get on your keyboard, whichever you prefer.

You can pick a prompt if you like. Pick a subject that you just want to start writing about. Or you can just set your mind at ease, and just write whatever comes to mind. But you have to do it as fast as reasonably possible. No pauses, no breaks, no breathers, and for the full allotted time you have to just keep writing. Don't hit the backspace, don't delete. There's no editing in here. When the right word won't come to you, you can either keep repeating the word that you just wrote again, again, again, again, until it comes. Or "um, um, um," you just keep writing that until the word that you want comes to your brain, and it will. Then when you're ready, you can move on. Type that word and just keep going.

If you get totally stuck, just skip the word and keep writing. Then let's say you get to the end of a sentence, and you just don't know what to write next. Or you're kind of stuck. Ask yourself at the end of that sentence, "Now, why do I think that way? Why is that the best thing to talk about in my book? Well, if that's true, what else is true? If that's true, is the opposite false?" You can actually type the questions as you're going, and then type your answer to those questions. You don't look back, you don't delete, you don't correct misspellings, you just continue to write until that timer goes off.

The key to free writing is to write as fast as you possibly can. That will help you to push past your internal editor, which we all have. Because you have a million ideas swimming about in your brain, colliding, generally being useless. So you need to get those ideas down on paper so you can think about them properly. The problem is, your internal editor has a habit of stopping those ideas before you manage to type them out. So the thoughts, they flit across your brain, but your fingers are paused on the keyboard and you think, "No, I'm not going to write that."

In this exercise, it'll be too late for your internal editor to stop you. Because you're just writing as fast as you can. As you're writing this gobbledygook nonsense, you'll stumble upon some of the most brilliant ideas. Ideas that never would have made it on paper had you not been typing so fast. So just tell your brain that it's okay. If you do this a few times, your brain will start to get it. Your internal editor will relax, knowing that it's only gonna last for 20 minutes. If you push past that 20 minutes, you probably won't get much more out of it. So don't push yourself past the 20.

The critical piece is using that timer. Nothing will kickstart your focus like setting a timer, and just getting busy. So use that timer. Any time you're doing free writing, researching, drafting, do it all with a timer running. It'll help you to stay focused, and know that when that timer gets done, you're free to stop.

The Pomodoro Technique

One of the techniques you probably heard of that can be very helpful is the Pomodoro Technique. You work in short blocks of time. Begin by setting your intentions. Set your timer and work for 25 minutes. Then you set the timer again, and take a five-minute break. Then you repeat. If you have the hour and 15 minutes, you do another 25 minutes writing and five minute break. If you have more time than that, you could do up to six blocks of time and still be productive. Anything beyond that, anything beyond three hours, you're probably not going to get a lot of good work out of yourself, unless you take a much longer break. I would start with that hour, and then move on after that.

Another good tool is tracking your progress. Set your weekly word count goal, and then create a spreadsheet, or on your calendar every day mark how many words you wrote, something so that you know that you're on track. It's amazing. Without tracking things, we think that we've done much better than we have. So make certain that you track your progress, so you really know if you're going to be on track.

Summary

Prioritize the habits you need to become a successful author. Set a weekly word count goal, and create a system to track your progress. Establish you're writing routines by deciding where, when, and what devices you'll write. Including what software you'll use for those writings. Make sure that you do free writing before each writing session. Even five minutes will help. Use a timer to write in 25 minute blocks of time, with five minute breaks in-between.

BEST DAMN MARKETING TOOL EVER

"SUCCESSFUL PEOPLE ARE SUCCESSFUL BECAUSE THEY FORM THE HABITS OF DOING THOSE THINGS THAT FAILURES DON'T LIKE TO DO."
~ ALBERT GRAY

CHECK OUT THE LIST OF RESOURCES AT
INSPIREDPRESSPUBLISHER.COM/RESOURCES

Chapter Eight

BEYOND THE FIRST DRAFT

Now consider the other elements of your book. Let's look at several important sections.

COPYRIGHT

Simply including @Copyright protects your work. Copyright is a form of protection grounded in the U.S. Constitution and granted by law for original works of authorship fixed in a tangible medium of expression. Copyright covers both published and unpublished works.

A literary work is a work that explains, describes, or narrates a particular subject, theme, or idea through the use of narrative, descriptive, or explanatory text, rather than dialog or dramatic action.

If you do not register your works you are not allow you to go after anyone for copyright infringement. Registration is recommended for a number of reasons. Many choose to register their works because they wish to have the facts of their copyright on the public record and have a certificate of registration. Registered works may be eligible for statutory damages and attorney's fees in successful litigation. Finally, if registration occurs within five years of publication, it is considered *prima facie* evidence in a court of law. For more information visit copyright.gov.

THE FOREWORD

Try to get an expert in your field to contribute a foreword. It is very prestigious when a person with a recognizable name or a recognizable title is connected with your book. Contact one of your peers about writing your foreword. Help this person by writing it yourself to demonstrate what you are looking for. Experts are busy people, and it is always easier for them to edit than to create.

It is doubtful that many people read the foreword, but they will notice who wrote it. The fact is, most readers turn directly to the action. You may wish to note "Foreword by..." on the cover if that important name will help sell books.

If you include a foreword, note the correct spelling; it is not "forward". It is the "word" that comes before the text.

TESTIMONIALS

Testimonials, endorsements, and excerpts from reviews can be added to the first pages of books. These are important sales pieces so always include any testimonials or endorsements your book receives right in the front matter. Put two or three of the best testimonials that space will allow on the back cover and the balance of them in this front section.

DEDICATION PAGE

Some authors like to praise their family for supporting them during the book-writing journey. You may dedicate your book to whomever you wish, or skip the section altogether. It is totally your preference.

ACKNOWLEDGMENTS

These can be a great sales tool. List everyone who helped you prepare your manuscript and book. People love to see their name in print, and each will become a fan that will assist in spreading the word about your book. As you are writing be sure to keep a running list of those who have helped to make certain no one is left out.

Now for the rear matter. Continue to ensure your work is considered to be professional by including these items in the back of the book. They are often left out of a self-published book. You may decide they are not necessary, but you should be aware of them and try to include them.

THE APPENDIX

This section contains important lists and other information. It may be composed of several sections. As you collect information on your subject, add resources to this section. Add other books, reports, associations, conferences, podcasts, suppliers and so on. A book with a large appendix often becomes a valuable reference that people *have* to own.

THE GLOSSARY

This is an alphabetically arranged dictionary of terms that are peculiar to the subject of your book. Some authors like to save space and simplify use by combining the glossary and the index.

THE BIBLIOGRAPHY

Here is where you list all the sources and reference materials used in writing your book. Especially if you include quotes, charts, and lots of facts, you may footnote them in the text, but always include the full reference here.

THE INDEX

This section aids the reader in locating specific information within the book's pages. It is particularly important in reference works. Many librarians will not purchase books without indexes, so plan on including an index. The index is at the very end of the book to make it easy to locate. Again, whether you include it or not depends on why you are writing and how you intend to use your book.

THE COVER

You've worked so hard on creating a work that people will love. Now all you need is something to convince people they should read what you've created. The cover of your book is the first thing potential readers see. Though creating a book cover may seem like haphazard combinations of fonts, colors, and images that just sit nicely with its creator, there is science and mechanism behind the creation of a book cover.

Most people know the commonly used expression "Don't judge a book by its cover." The fact of the matter is, your book *will* be judged by its cover. Try as you might to fight this nugget of truth, there isn't any getting around it. Your book cover is a visual representative of what is written on the pages inside. Since the cover of a book is the very first thing that meets the reader's eye, the message it conveys should be clear and should align with the story unfolding within.

In the words of accomplished book cover designer Chip Kidd, "A book cover is a distillation of the content, almost like what your book would look like as a haiku."

If you haven't done so already, you will need to have your book cover created. Most nonfiction books are 6 X 9 and will require a jpg and pdf format.

Know Your Audience

The design of a book cover is a science as well as a fine art. Different aesthetics will appeal to different types of people. When you're in the process of designing your book cover, your target audience needs to be taken into account.

Your book cover is, essentially, a marketing strategy to your audience. The words on the inside should have everything to do with your color scheme, typography, and format. Ask yourself what your audience should expect from your book, and then make sure the cover is designed appropriately to give what the reader expects from you.

Font Type Matters

The font in which your book title will be displayed is equally as important as the rest of your cover. If we're being realistic, you should know that no one likes Comic Sans. If this were a do's and don'ts list, using Comic Sans or Papyrus fonts would definitely be at the top of the don't list. The font you choose should grab the reader's attention, but it's a good idea to stick with only one type of font, or two at the most.

Remember the Back Cover

With all the talk about fonts, colors, and imagery on the front cover, you don't want to leave out the back cover. The back cover is made for a short blurb or small description of your book. This is a sales pitch to make potential readers understand why they need to buy *your* book.

The goal of the back-cover blurb is to leave the reader wanting more. When you write the blurb, give the reader enough information to grab their attention, but don't give away too much. Leave them with some vague idea of what's to come. You want to compel them to open it and see the resolution for themselves.

Of course, keeping the reader's attention is almost as important as gaining it. You don't want to lose the reader's attention before they even leave the back cover. A general rule to go by is to write in short paragraphs so it's easier for the reader to scan.

Say what you will, but a great example of an effective back cover blurb comes from Stephanie Mayer's *Twilight*:

"About three things I was absolutely positive.

First, Edward was a vampire.

Second, there was a part of him — and I didn't know how dominant that part might be — that thirsted for my blood.

And the third, I was unconditionally and irrevocably In love with him."

Get Professional Help

While all the above are good pieces of advice to follow, you should get professional help. Professional designers can help you appeal to your target audience with the right colors and images that are attractive to that audience. An experienced artist will have more knowledge about the things that draw readers in. If you have plans of your own for your book cover, remember that just because it is appealing to you doesn't mean it will appeal to everyone.

If you want a good design but don't have a few thousand dollars to shell out to an independent artist, there are still some options for you. You can still find some professional help on websites like *Fiverr* or *Upwork* for a lower cost.

Hiring a professional doesn't mean you have to give up your ideas entirely. Find artwork that appeals to you, and that can reveal your aesthetic to your artist. Take a look at other book covers similar to yours and even some that aren't. Take note of the things you think are effective and what isn't. Communicating with your artist will help you be able to achieve the perfect look that will satisfy you as well as the reader.

Moving On

One of the most important things for you to consider is hiring an editor. The one thing that will destroy your reputation is a book filled with errors. Set yourself apart from a lot of self-published authors and look like the rock star that you are. A good editor will clean up grammar, spelling and formatting. As well as, making suggestions for where it can be improved.

Typically, an editor charges by the page or the word.

A developmental editor provides a thorough and in-depth edit of your entire manuscript. It is an edit of all the elements of your writing, from single words and the phrasing of individual sentences, to overall structure and style.

After a round of developmental editing, a manuscript can change substantially; for a first-time author, accepting direct and honest feedback can be a difficult experience. Just remember good developmental editing will improve your work. Once your manuscript has been cut, reshaped, revised, and developed, it will be ready for a copy edit and proofread.

Publishing

Once your manuscript is finished it is time to finalize all of the details. You will either go completely with the self-publishing plan or hire a company that will handle all of the details and still allow you to maintain all royalties from your work.

Those final details include obtaining an ISBN number and then applying to the Library of Congress. This is a three-step process: you purchase your ISBN number and then you apply to the Library of Congress; when you receive that number you go back to the ISBN number and finish up your listing. Your listing will include your title, description, and cover image. Once you have those numbers to include in the manuscript, now you can have it formatted for print as well as digital publishing.

Benefits of publishing eBooks with Amazon KDP

- Rights: Keep control of your rights and set your own list prices. Make changes to your books at any time.
- Get to market fast: Set up your book in minutes, and it will appear on Kindle stores worldwide.

- Royalties: Earn up to 70% royalty on sales to customers in the US, Canada, UK, Germany, India, France, Italy, Spain, Japan, Brazil, Mexico, Australia and more. Enroll in KDP Select and earn more money through Kindle Unlimited and the Kindle Owners' Lending Library.

Take the formatted documents and upload them to Amazon https://kdp.amazon.com/ and simply follow the steps.

This will give you the option for print on demand and save you the need to purchase 100 copies at a time. However, you can purchase copies at a discounted rate to use in your marketing.

Selecting your categories and keywords are an important aspect for getting found on Amazon. You can also benefit from a successful book in your genre by using the book title as one of your keywords. When choosing your categories, select two different categories and subcategories. Don't choose two subcategories under the same category. Review the bestsellers list for each specific category and use the subcategories that will help you rank at the top of your selected genre.

Find a category that is not very competitive to help you reach the top. Find the book rankings by going to your chosen categories and clicking on the top books. Then look under the product details on the page. If the book ranks 5000 or higher, then the category is a good option.

BEST DAMN MARKETING TOOL EVER

"OUR BUSINESS IN LIFE IS NOT TO GET AHEAD OF OTHERS, BUT TO GET AHEAD OF OURSELVES—TO BREAK OUR OWN RECORDS, TO OUTSTRIP OUR YESTERDAY BY OUR TODAY."
~ STEWART B. JOHNSON ~

CHECK OUT THE LIST OF RESOURCES AT
INSPIREDPRESSPUBLISHER.COM/RESOURCES

Chapter Nine

PRE-PUBLICATION

Your book promotion begins long before you are published. Use the following tips and suggestions to begin promoting your book while you are still in the writing phase. A good time frame to begin is at least 6-9 months before your book is ready for publication.

- If you are building a business as a speaker and author then you need a dedicated website.
- If you are using your book as a marketing tool to promote your business then you need a landing page where you can begin to build your email list by offering the first chapter of your book in exchange for their email address.
- Also be sure to create an author's page on Amazon at authorscentral.amazon.com.

Develop your book cover in advance. Narrow the choices to two or three options and share these across social media asking your fans to vote. Post samples of your cover on your blog or email list and ask for feedback. This will not only help you choose an attractive cover, it will drum up attention about your book that is soon to be available.

Pre-Publication Research

Research for pre-publication should include:

- Determine your pricing strategy
- If you know other authors in your genre, ask them about cross promotion. Goodreads.com is a good place to connect.
- Ask for beta-readers to give feedback on your book (Facebook 6 reviewers)
- Brainstorm keywords for your book
- Find hashtags used by readers in your genre/topics
- Find Facebook and LinkedIn groups and pages that relate to your book. Begin engaging with the group.
- Find Google+ communities related to your genre
- Find forums dedicated to your genre
- Find blogs that review books in your genre
- Listen to the Novel Marketing Podcast.

Where to Find Reviews for Your Book

The Book Blogger List - (http://bookbloggerlist.com) This site features a large database of book blogger sites. It is organized by genre.

The YA Book Blog Directory - (http://yabookblogdirectory.blogspot.ca) This directory focuses solely on the wildly popular Young Adult genre. The site features a comprehensive listing of YA book review blog

Story Cartel - (https://storycartel.com) Here, authors can submit their books for free in exchange for honest reviews from readers.

Directory of Book Bloggers on Pinterest– (http://www.mandyboles.com/2012/01/directory-of-book-bloggers-on-pinterest/) Curated by

Mandy Boles, this site keeps an up-to-date listing of the many book bloggers active on the social media site Pinterest.

Kate Tilton's Book Bloggers - (http://katetilton.com/kate-tiltons-book-bloggers/) Kate Tilton keeps a smaller, but accurate list of book bloggers who will review titles by indie authors.

The Indie View (http://www.theindieview.com/indie-reviewers/) Simply one of the web's most complete listings of independent book reviewers.

Goodreads - (http://www.goodreads.com) Goodreads is a terrific place for authors to promote their books, and it offers indie writers the chance to exchange reviews with their peers.

Self-Publishing Review — (http://www.selfpublishingreview.com/about/) For a fee, authors can receive an impartial, editorial book review. The site also offers paid editing services.

IndieReader — (http://indiereader.com/authorservices/service-sample/) IndieReader, which exists as a consumer guide for readers of self-published authors, offers professional book reviews for a fee.

Social Media Exposure

Begin using social media prior to publication so you can build your audience. All posts, photographs, images, and videos can be shared by visitors with their friends or other networks. This can help you build a following of interested readers through the shares on social networks.

Select the social networks that you prefer and that your target market is using. When authors place promotional posts on social networks, they get instant exposure on a global scale. The author can gauge the response of readers by checking the feedback posted by readers on the social network posts. The feedback across social networks will help you feel the pulse of the reader before the book is published. Authors can communicate with potential readers and improve their books before they publish.

Promotion on Goodreads

Goodreads is a popular social network connected to Amazon and dedicated to books, their authors, and readers. To begin promoting your book on Goodreads, follow these steps:

1. Sign up for a Goodreads reader account.
2. Fill in the profile and add a professional picture.
3. Set up an author page on Goodreads.
4. Find friends from social networks or email friends who have signed up on Goodreads and start inviting them to read the book and provide a review.
5. Join groups or create a Goodreads group.
6. Ask followers of the book on other social networks or readers on Goodreads to list the book on the Listopia section of Goodreads.
7. Find authors of similar books and target their fans with an advertisement of the book.
8. Raise awareness of the book by giving away books on the book giveaways section of Goodreads.
9. Host a discussion about the book. Goodreads has a discussion hosting option that will help increase awareness among readers about the book.
10. Connect the blog and website to Goodreads to help readers learn more about the book by visiting the website.

11. Put a Goodreads widget on the website or blog. The widget will update the website or blog when any activity is performed on Goodreads. Google is impressed by activity on Goodreads and increases the search ranking of the author.
12. Link the Goodreads account with other social network accounts like Facebook or Twitter.
13. Ask fans and readers to review the book. Positive and negative reviews boost the popularity of the book.
14. Add books that the author has read to the author account and like reviews of these books written by other readers.
15. Rate other books and post reviews.

BEST DAMN MARKETING TOOL EVER

"PEOPLE CAN'T READ A BOOK IF THEY DON'T KNOW IT EXISTS. ALL AUTHORS NEED TO DO MARKETING, REGARDLESS OF HOW THEY PUBLISHED."
~ JO LINSDELL

CHECK OUT THE LIST OF RESOURCES AT
INSPIREDPRESSPUBLISHER.COM/RESOURCES

Chapter Ten

GETTING NOTICED IN A NOISY WORLD

This chapter is all about promotional ideas to get your book out before the masses, to harvest reviews, and to generally promote the book.

Build an Email List

Make certain you have a link in the front of your book driving traffic to your website to capture their email. You can offer a companion to your book, like a checklist, worksheets, or video expanding the information offered in your book.

Set up an email capture on your landing page using a service like Mailchimp.com or ActiveCampaign.com. Write 3 - 5 email follow-ups to encourage your readers to schedule an appointment with you, book your services, purchase your book or other products, or some other desired action.

Harvest Reviews from Amazon

Invest at least two weeks and focus on getting reviews. People don't trust a book that has only one review. Here is a great plan to gather in reviews from Amazon.

Add your book to Amazon for Kindle for 99 cents. Don't publicize it yet. Ask anyone who is willing to purchase the book at this basement price, read it, and write you a review. Because Amazon knows they actually purchased the book, their review becomes verified. A verified review has a lot more weight than a non-verified review. You need at least 10, but 20 or more would be better.

Book Pricing Promotion

After gathering in at least 10-20 reviews, set up a promotional event on Amazon where your book will be free for 24-48 hours. Inflate the book price initially because Amazon will show how much the buyer will save, making your book have a higher perceived value. So, even if you plan on settling on a price of $10.99 for your book, list it now at $18.99, for example. It looks as if the buyer will save more getting in now on the limited-time free deal.

At the end of the promotion, put your book back at 99 cents for a day or two. This will help with those that missed your promotion. If it is only 99 cents, other readers will more than likely purchase it. The higher you can get your book in the free charts, the more eyeballs will see your book. It can be as high as hundreds a minute. Keep your book at 99 cents for one week. Then slowly raise the price, bumping the price up one dollar every 5-7 days until you reach your final price.

Every time you raise the price, put a notice at the beginning of the description.

"I have discounted the price of my book for the next 5 days during the launch. Grab your copy now before the price goes up to the final amount of $12.99 on Friday (11/3)."

You can run different price increase promotions for print and Kindle versions, since your Kindle version will cost less.

Spend money to promote the promotion if at all possible. Amazon appreciates those who can show they can drive external traffic to their book, and they reward them. Drive as much traffic as possible during the promotion time frame so you can dominate the categories you have chosen for your book.

Speakers Sheet

If you are a speaker, coach, or consultant, writing a book can help you to get more business and increase your fees. A book is the best damn marketing tool you can use.

If your book is going to open doors for you to get speaking gigs or interviews, then you will want a speaker's sheet developed that you can send when requesting the gig. Finding those speaking gigs can be the result of a Google search for something like "conferences in Ohio" or "association conferences in Tennessee."

You can also use tools like https://myspeakingagent.com to find opportunities.

Getting interviewed on podcasts, radio, and even television is greatly increased by having a book. Today, approximately one in five adults in the US listen to podcasts.

Remember you are competing for the interview with hundreds or even thousands. The key to getting the interview is to be a great guest. Provide value for the Podcaster's audience and make them look good. Preparation is everything.

Podcasts allow you to get exposure to a very targeted and engaged audience. They will drive traffic to your website and help people to almost immediately decide if they like you. As well as build relationships with influencers in your industry.

Finding the right podcasts is fairly easy as there are multiple podcast directories: Stitcher, Spreaker, Google Play but the largest is iTunes. iTunes reported in 2013 they there were over 1 billion podcasts on the platform. You can also do a Google search Google search: [your topic] inurl:/podcast/. The search results will only return podcasts.

One more option is Radio Guest List. Radio Guest List can connect you to thousands of media outlets including podcasts, radio shows, and even television producers with experts and PR firms who are looking for exposure. Sign up for their free emails, they will send you specific interview opportunities. You can then email the hosts and producers your speaker sheet and pitch to appear on their show. If you reach out on Facebook or LinkedIn, your pitch should be personalized and should simply ask if they are looking for more guests and that you would love to be considered. If you receive a positive response you can ask for their email address and then send your speakers sheet or offer a copy of your book, but don't be surprised if they don't read it.

If you are reaching out through email you can offer more details. Here is what you should send:

- Your name, contact details, and link to online assets (website, social media, book, etc.)
- Your bio and relevant credentials and achievements (to show credibility)
- Social proof (other interviews you've done, connections you have in common, etc.)
- Your one-sheet or media kit (if you have one). Your media kit can include a list of questions around your book that they may use during the interview.

Once booked, be a great guest. Prepare for the show, use your headset, and reduce the background noise. Don't attempt to multi-task; make the podcast your priority.

Outreach

One more option is to reach out to those who hire speakers on LinkedIn, ask them to connect with you, and then send a thank you and let them know you are looking for speaking gigs.

If you are looking for individual clients the same LinkedIn process can be used, but the follow up thank-you could offer them the first chapter of your book. Drive them to your landing page to give their email in exchange for the first chapter.

Take your networking to the next level and use your book as a business card to introduce yourself to prospects in your local market. When was the last time you threw a book away? Your prospects won't either; they will put it on a shelf somewhere in their office and every time they see the book, they will think of you.

You could also offer training or workshops locally, teaching the principles in your book.

When giving speeches, sell your books to the audience, and at the full price. Who wouldn't want an autographed book and the instant gratification of leaving with a copy of your book?

Your book launch strategy could include offering bonuses when someone purchases your book. Bonuses could include reports, whitepapers, digital workbooks, audio recordings, training videos, checklists, templates, or any other downloadable content.

Your launch announcements should begin about a week after your book is published. You may need a launch team to help. People who will help spread the word, family and friends, LinkedIn connections, people of your email list and social media followers. If you recommend a person or company in your book, be certain you notify them. Anyone who contributed to your book should be on your announcement list.

Develop a local media list to send your press releases. And you can purchase a list at http://gebbiepress.com/ to expand your reach.

Look for groups that have your target market in them on Facebook and LinkedIn.

Prepare in advance all social media posts, email content, and any other content you are using to announce the launch. You can schedule most of this in advance.

If you are interested in speaking, be sure to add a speaker page to your website with the same information you used on your speaker's sheet, including video clips if you have them.

Plan a launch party if your business is local where you can sign books. Use PayPal or Stripe on your phone or tablet to process credit card payments. Be sure to go live on Instagram, Facebook, or YouTube. On launch day go live on Facebook. After the recording is added to your Facebook page boost the post to get in front of your target market.

BEST DAMN MARKETING TOOL EVER

"THE SIZE OF YOUR AUDIENCE IS MORE IMPORTANT THAN THE SIZE OF YOUR BOOK"
— BERNARD KELVIN CLIVE

CHECK OUT THE LIST OF RESOURCES AT
INSPIREDPRESSPUBLISHER.COM/RESOURCES

Chapter Eleven

TOOLS EVERY WRITER CAN USE

Every writer has their favorite tools that make the process of sharing our thoughts with the world easier and more appealing. No doubt, you have your own list and have read through countless others. This list of 18 tools *every* writer can use highlights simple tools that practically anyone can use. Beginners and up can find valuable help to boost their writing game right from the start, with little to no training or study.

So, if you're new to the game and wondering where to begin using tools, and what tools to begin with, this handy list is your starting point. Examine each tool and see how it can help you. Everyone looks for certain preferences, and some value certain features more highly than others. Try each tool and use what fits for you.

Brainstorming Tools

These content writing tools help you generate, brainstorm, and organize your ideas.

Ideaflip

Have you ever tried writing down every idea that pops into your head, and then organizing them into some sort of categories for writing? Sounds kind of stupid, huh? Instead of creating a list of jumbled thoughts and creating content around it, you can use Ideaflip. This tool provides a visual, interactive environment that enables you to record, manage, and develop your ideas. The user interface allows you to do anything that will help your ideas spring to life.

HubSpot's Blog Topic Generator

Instead of using random ideas that may appeal to no one, HubSpot's Blog Topic Generator allows you to use up to three keywords to generate ideas more focused around topics that are important to your audience. The tool takes your keywords and generates a long list of subjects you use right away or that can further help direct your research.

Portent's Content Idea Generator

This headline generator can inspire you to change the way you initially intended to deliver your ideas. To create a topic, enter any word related to your keyword or idea into the search field. You can update search results as many times as necessary until the topic and title is a perfect match for your idea.

Editing and Writing Tools

Every writer needs editing and style correcting tools. Writing tools should free you from clutter, help with writer's block, and help us catch most of the typos and grammar mistakes we regularly make.

Scrivener

Scrivener is a typewriter, ring binder, scrapbook, research assistant, and publishing tool all rolled into one exceptional package. It is a desktop program that combines word processor and project management into one all-inclusive package. Write your material, your way, and keep tabs on all your ideas as they come. Available for Mac and Windows users.

Grammarly

Grammarly is arguably the best spelling and grammar checker available. It will easily spot errors other apps can't, and will also help you optimize your text and make it more readable. Plugins are available for Microsoft Word and internet browsers as well. Grammarly keeps all those troublesome grammar rules in its head so you can write with freedom and make accurate corrections later.

Hemingway

Writing for a particular audience or reading level? Hemingway highlights sentences and phrases that are too complex, suggests eliminating excessive adverbs, and turning passive voice constructions into active voice. It even shows a text's readability score. The counter feature shows the total number of words, characters, paragraphs, and sentences so you can tweak a text's structure or word count. This tool is available for both PC and Mac.

Copyscape

Copyscape provides the most powerful and popular online plagiarism detection solutions, ranked #1 by independent tests. Copyscape is trusted by millions of writers and website owners to check the originality of their new content, prevent duplicate content, and search for copies of existing content online.

Power Thesaurus

Power Thesaurus is a free thesaurus app which is crowdsourced, eliminating any ads. Its user interface is streamlined and elegant, and the app itself is always keeping up with all the latest developments in linguistics. Boost your language usage with Power Thesaurus.

Planning Tools

Keep your writing process on track with to-do lists, calendars, workflow organizing, file sharing, and more.

Wunderlist

Wunderlist is a digital organizer that can keep your ideas well-structured and remind you of other necessary tasks. It can also transform your emails into to-do lists, move them between folders, and add notices. Share your lists with others, or print them out with a single click.

Google Calendar

Almost everyone uses Gmail, and many use Google Calendar for planning. Why not turn it into a daily planner for your writing and publishing tasks, too? Schedule posts for exact times and dates, and write down topic ideas for upcoming posts. The calendar allows you to make to-do lists and schedule events. In addition, sync your calendar on your mobile device for on-the-go organization.

Dropbox

What can be better than online file storage accessible from any device? Drobox allows you to store your files and share them with others as well. Plus, Dropbox is ideal for exchanging large files like videos and working jointly on the same projects.

Shareist

Save and organize links, images, video URLs into your projects.
 Notes and tags are available. Shareist is a web app to keep all your content centralized and organized into projects. Share it privately with your team, clients, or publicly on social media.

BEST DAMN MARKETING TOOL EVER

"ALL OF US POSSESS A READING VOCABULARY AS BIG AS A LAKE BUT DRAW FROM A WRITING VOCABULARY AS SMALL AS A POND. THE GOOD NEWS IS THAT THE ACTS OF SEARCHING AND GATHERING ALWAYS EXPAND THE NUMBER OF USABLE WORDS."
~ ROY PETER CLARK

CHECK OUT THE LIST OF RESOURCES AT
INSPIREDPRESSPUBLISHER.COM/RESOURCES

REFERENCES

Seth Godin
https://www.sethgodin.com

Client Heartbeat
https://www.clientheartbeat.com

Brand Advocates, Rob Ruggetta
http://robfuggetta.com/about-the-book/

Tanya Hall, CEO of Greanleaf Book Group
http://www.greenleafbookgroup.com

From Frazzled to Freedom" Julie Starr Hook
https://www.amazon.com/Julie-Starr-Hook/e/B00JQI18VW/

Erika Anderson
https://www.forbes.com/sites/erikaandersen/#255839313bef

David Niu
https://www.tinypulse.com/blog/author/david-niu

Brian Tracy
https://www.briantracy.com

Spanish Proverb
http://thinkexist.com/quotation/habits_are_first_cobwebs-then_cables/341528.html

If you are ready to write and finish your book schedule a consultation at www.inspiredpresspublisher.com